Duck Soup
Vignettes of Country Life

By

Inge Perreault

Large Print Edition

Photography by Roland Perreault

ISBN: 0-75962-145-4

This book is printed on acid free paper.

1stBooks - rev. 7/10/01

This book is dedicated to my family, my husband Roland, my sons Marc and Eric as well as to my grandparents and parents who instilled in me early on the love of all living things.

I would also like to thank a very special group of people whose unconditional love and encouragement were instrumental in pursuing my dream, They know who they are!

TABLE OF CONTENTS

MY DONI

My Doni was born literally out of despair and in hope for a better future. During the deepest depression, caused by our then so very difficult financial situation in the midst of the last recession, grew the search for a new value system. A renewed and healing connection with nature caused us in the spring of 1988 to acquire some duck, pheasant and chicken eggs at the local game farm. With the help of an incubator, which we borrowed from our neighbor who is a science teacher, we began in many ways a new journey and direction in our lives.

Without meaning to sound presumptuous or plain silly, I must admit that the following experiences have not only contributed immense joy in one way, but have also brought us to appreciate once more those aspects of life, which our modern world does not seem to value enough any longer. Yet, they are so very important to our humanness.

So allow me to start at the very beginning of our adventure and share with you the wonderful happiness a little feathered creature brought into our lives.

After placing the eggs carefully into the incubator, we made sure that during the following 20 days they were turned daily

1

and that the humidity level was proper. Then, on day 21, when I gently opened the incubator, I noticed one of the eggs moving all by itself. I was astounded to say the least. Here was a sign of life, the miracle of creation right in front of my eyes. I will never forget the feeling of awe I experienced at that very moment.

During the next two days the egg moved with increasing frequency and then, one night, we heard at first a hardly audible peeping, which gradually grew louder and louder. The funniest thing was that we were actually able to converse with this egg. If we imitated the peeping twice, there would be two peeps coming back. All possible combinations were tried and each time the answer would be correct, whether five times, three, six or four, each time it would repeat our amount of peeps. You can imagine what a ridiculous sight it must have been, two grown-ups and two young boys having a conversation with an egg. We found it absolutely fascinating.

On day 24 our little duck decided to leave it's confinement. Entering this world was not easy. Even with my help the hatching process took almost all morning until the duckling finally lay totally exhausted and wet in the incubator.

When the children returned from school they were overjoyed and, since we did not know whether we had succeeded in hatching a male or female duck, we named it in good American fashion "Donald". Later, when we found out that she was a member of the weaker but more intelligent sex, (I am a little prejudiced in this matter) we simply abbreviated her name to "Doni". She was the only one of twenty eggs which hatched and made it into this world. I instantly knew that what we had here was a duck with a mission!

Doni was the most adorable little creature you can imagine. Her tiny little bill, the fluffy brownish down feathers and those little black feet conquered our hearts in no time at all. Since she had encountered me first and ducks imprint, she considered me to be her "mother". She literally followed me everywhere on quick little feet, crying bitterly if she could not see me. Our son Eric found a good-sized carton, a heat lamp and a warm old towel which were stashed under his desk and became Doni's first home. We gave her food and a little dish of drinking water into which, in typical duck fashion, she jumped immediately with total abandonment. Just in case she felt lonely, we provided her with a little stuffed animal. She used it at night to snuggle with and it later followed her into the garden shed, which meanwhile had been converted into a chicken coop. There she kept it for many years, dragging it around with her bill and sitting on it if she was not feeling well. By then it was tattered and barely recognizable but in a way it was her security blanket. Ducks do catch colds once in a while or get laryngitis as well as sinus infections, although in general wild ducks are a lot more disease resistant than domesticated fowl.

Eric had cut a little exit door into the front of the carton which was her first home, and it could be lowered like a drawbridge. Doni would come walking out almost like a little toy soldier, proudly and full of life. Since we were dealing with an extremely intelligent duck, she learned in no time at all the location of the door and would hammer with her little bill against it furiously, as soon as someone entered the room, in order to be allowed to leave her confinement. At night, when the family would sit together in the family room watching TV or talking over the day's events, Doni had to be part of it all. She would climb on the boys, sit on their shoulders or on mine, pull on our earlobes and eventually fall, totally exhausted, fast asleep on an old towel in my lap.

As the days grew warmer, Doni developed into an adorable "teenager". During the day we now left her outside in the enclosed chicken yard, and sometimes we would take her on little walks down to our stream in the woods. It was a beautiful spring. The trees were fully clad in their fresh green leaves by now, the skunk cabbage in full growth and soft moss cushioning the sound of our feet. Only occasionally the silence was broken by one of us stepping on a dry branch or old leaves from the previous fall. Just try to imagine, two adults, two young boys and a little duck marching through field and woods, over rock, fallen tree limbs and mossy ground, finally reaching the stream which was heaven to Doni. Once in a while I would pack her up in a little cushioned wicker basket to make it easier on her little legs, and she would stick her head out in great anticipation of the pleasurable experience that lay ahead. She never wanted to stay there by herself though. As soon as we were out of sight we could hear her worried quacking and calling. She was overjoyed when she caught sight of us again. Spring turned into a wonderful summer! I had planted honeysuckle by the door of the coop which took off like a tropical vine and the fragrance was intoxicating. The window of the coop had been adorned by a flower box planted with colorful petunias, geraniums and hanging vinca vines. The path leading from the house to the chicken coop was now clearly marked with a copper sign my husband had given me for my birthday, showing several ducks with an inscription underneath reading "Duck Crossing".

By now Doni was allowed to accompany me into the swimming pool although she had her little pond in the chicken yard, which had been my Mother's Day gift from my older son. Overshadowed by a small elderberry bush as protective cover from birds of prey, she enjoyed it thoroughly, but going for a swim with me was her very special treat. The two of us would swim and dive, tease each other and she just loved climbing on my back while I was swimming, preening my hair gently. Ever so often she would look at me mischievously, dive and give me a little pinch on the bottom, then show up at the other end of the pool looking very proud of herself and seeming happy at having gotten the better of me once again. I could swear there were times she was actually laughing at me, for the sounds she made were only made when had had been up to no good.

One night, my husband will never forget it, she went to him when he was sitting in the grass, climbed into his arms and fell fast asleep. In general she was crazy about him. There was great excitement when he returned from work. Her entire little body would actually quiver with anticipation as soon as she heard his voice. Here was Papa and he had to be welcomed home with her tender preening efforts of his hair and face. Incidentally, ducks have an incredible sense of hearing. Every time I returned home from taking the dog for a walk I would hear her calling me from far away. Her greeting call was very different from other sounds she made. Actually, every time I would leave the house and return, I was duly welcomed by her calls. My neighbor told me that she knew exactly about my comings and goings just from hearing Doni, and there is quite a distance between our two houses.

Summer was almost over and oftentimes Doni seemed lonely. Even though she shared the chicken yard and coop with 4 chickens (over whom she ruled in a rather dictatorial manner), after all she considered herself almost human, something was missing. In the fall the boys tried to teach her how to fly, but unfortunately they had as little success with their efforts as I did. The landings were at times not exactly smooth and even though she would glide across half the yard, she never really did get off the ground. In order to learn how to fly properly she would have needed a real duck mother I assume, we just did not have the right technique. I tried to be her mother to the best of my ability, she followed me everywhere, even out to the mail box to get the mail. Many a passerby would ask me in amazement why it was, that this duck was so tame? Some people, after having seen us together, even showed up at my doorstep with children or grandchildren in tow, asking me if the kids could

meet the duck. Naturally I always obliged, for I felt here was a good lesson for children, teaching them that animals should be treated kindly in general and likewise showing them to appreciate the joy they can add to our lives.

One particular activity Doni absolutely loved was standing by my side while I was working in the garden, where she would eagerly search for worms or slugs as I was turning over the ground. Another of her favorite things to do was follow me into the house, where she knew exactly the location of the refrigerator, eagerly anticipating a piece of lettuce which she would gobble up quickly and then wash down with water from the dog's water dish.

Because she was a duck with truly great intellect, she immediately recognized that our retired greyhound Buck was a pacifist (actually a coward) and loved him therefore all the more. After nibbling at his toenails she actually once hopped on his back. I always regretted not having a camera handy to take a snapshot; it would have made a great picture.

But let us return to her feelings of loneliness. After the first winter she became downright melancholic, and so we decided to venture out in search of a mate. After several rather unsuccessful attempts to catch a male duck at the local game farm (with permission of the warden of course) we gave up and let our fingers do the walking. Eventually we found a farm about an hour away from our house which specialized in the breeding of ducks. The owner was willing to sell us a male duck at the bargain price of $10. In June, when Doni had grown into a pretty young duck lady, we returned with Ralph, like her a mix of Mallard and Indian Runner. A good-looking young lad but not too bright, who immediately fell madly in love with Doni and

found in her his purpose for living; looking out for her and being very upset and jealous when Doni and I would have our little private times together. Since Doni was a young lady brought up with discriminating taste and good values, she showed a certain healthy skepticism towards his advances and it took a good three months, until she finally accepted him and they mated. He was absolutely faithful and took good care of her in adoring fashion. However, there were times, it was quite obvious to me, that he got on her nerves with his constant attention and quacking. She would follow me out of the chicken yard all too willingly, not even looking back once and totally ignoring his loud upset lamenting. Working in the vegetable garden, directly adjacent to the chicken yard, I had the opportunity on numerous occasions to observe arguments, when he would annoy her to the point that she would actually give him a good peck on the head, sending him for cover. Obviously that day she was not in the mood and needed her personal space.

In spite of her attachment to me and the family, she retained a healthy independence and had her very own ideas about things. This only made our relationship all the more special, since it was a sign of genuine trust between human and animal.

She loved to be picked up, brought up to my eye-level and gently nuzzle my face. At times we had little talks (in "duck" of course). When I quietly said "peep" her eyes would glaze over with happiness. It seemed to remind her of her childhood and she would answer me back in the same manner. Those were very special moments for us both; moments allowing us to build a bridge to each other which I considered a great gift. I felt terribly responsible for her well-being. Never in the past have I been able to develop such a close relationship with an animal and the experience has taught me a lot I find hard to put into words. They are felt more in the heart than in verbal expression. They are feelings of being close to nature, which in turn bring me closer to my very own core. It is amazing how significant a little duck can be.

Part II

The story about my little duck friend would not be complete without a description of the developments that followed. Actually, it will not be complete until she dies, but I cannot even think about that without getting teary-eyed. So I would just like to continue at the point the story ended a few years ago.

Doni and Ralph were a happy couple for about four years. They lived peacefully together with the chickens which, since their life span is considerably shorter, died off gradually, until finally only Henrietta was left. During the summertime Doni and Ralph swam in their little pond with Henrietta looking on while resting in the shade. Quite frequently I continued to take Doni swimming into the big pool, where we enjoyed ourselves immensely just clowning around. One of my favorite neighbors, a lovely Lady in her late seventies, often asked to join me for a dip on a hot day and insisted I bring Doni, since she loved swimming with her. To this day, she has a picture of Doni sitting on her tummy while she is floating on her back, tacked to her refrigerator.

The wintertime was often long for the poor animals, since those were years during which we experienced enormous quantities of snow. Thus they were confined to the coop for weeks. Several times a day I would bring out fresh lukewarm water as well as vegetable leftovers as little treats. The coop was filled regularly with a fresh layer of clean hay and on sunny days I would leave the big door to the coop open. All three of them, Doni, Ralph and Henrietta would find a sunny spot in the fresh hay and enjoy the warm rays of sunshine for as long as possible. Another summer went by and as I had done in the past, I would allow them to wander into the vegetable garden next to the chicken yard. Simply by removing a piece of fencing I was able to extend their space, allowing them to eat any leftovers. Doni, Ralph and Henrietta got into the habit of taking a nap under the currant bush in the corner of the garden and it was a peaceful existence for the three of them. Unfortunately, when I returned home from work one day, I noticed immediately upon getting out of the car that something was very wrong. Two huge hawks sat on a tree by the edge of the woods screeching at me furiously. With rather anxious feelings I ran towards the garden and was unable to locate Doni, Ralph or Henrietta. Immediately I searched the chicken coop, called for them but received no answer. Finally I discovered Doni and Henrietta pressed closely together and quite obviously traumatized in a corner of the yard by the duck pond and, after closer inspection of the vegetable garden, I came upon Ralph's lifeless body. The hawks had hacked his head open, shattering his skull. He must have died defending Doni and put up a valiant struggle, since there was blood everywhere. His body was still warm, apparently the incident had happened just a short time ago, and the hawks were angry at being deprived of a meal. I am absolutely certain he gave his life for Doni, instinctively, in spite of his general stupidity, he was always looking out for danger in order to protect his mate. Crying I picked him up, carried him away and quietly buried him in the same area which had become the resting place for our deceased chickens. It was a difficult thing to do, since I had gotten rather fond of him, even though he had annoyed me many times by not wanting to walk up the plank into the chicken coop at night without a major production.

It took Doni and Henrietta a long time to recover from the shock. For weeks they simply refused to leave the safety of the chicken coop. Who would dare say that animals do not think or remember. I will challenge anyone, for I have experienced and witnessed a lot of occasions which affirm the contrary.

Another winter came and Doni and Henrietta drew closer together. After all, by now they only had each other, and it was heartwarming to watch them, nestled next to each other in the hay: a middle-aged duck and a very old hen. In the spring Henrietta fell ill and Doni would not leave her side until she died. It was obvious that she mourned her old friend deeply, and now she was once again totally alone. Consequently we decided to find her a new husband and get some new chicks as well. Finally the chicken yard would be lively again.

This time we brought home a younger duck, named him Bob, but while she tolerated him, he never was able to replace her beloved Ralph. The age difference was too great, after all, it was a "September-May" relationship and they usually don't work out all that well, apparently even among animals. The points of interest change with age and so does the pace. The baby chicks grew into fine young hens and kept us, as well as our neighbors, in super colossal large eggs. When giving them away I would have to place a rubber band around the egg carton for the eggs were so sizeable, that an egg carton designed for extra-large would not even close. Once again there was a very peaceful atmosphere in the chicken yard. Everyone got along fine and seemed to be content.

Towards the end of the winter of 1996 Doni fell ill. At first I thought she merely caught a cold but then she became quite lethargic and when I took a closer look, I noticed that she had infected sinuses. So off to the veterinarian we went! Since most vets these days spend their time with cats and dogs, it must have been a special occasion for my veterinarian to examine a wild duck. Already in the waiting room she was quite the sensation. The entire staff as well as waiting owners with other pets just had to have a peek at her.

The veterinarian checked her out thoroughly, she weighed in at 4.5 pounds and my diagnosis was confirmed. (Maybe I should have become a veterinarian, a career which must be very rewarding.) Naturally the Doctor was astounded at just how tame the animal was and admired her close relationship with me, since I could handle her with great ease like any other pet without her fussing or getting upset. But then again, I was her mother! We left the office with a prescription for antibiotics which I had to give her twice a day. After two weeks there was a noticeable improvement. Doni, who had sat around listlessly for quite some time, suddenly reentered the pond and proceeded to groom herself. Bob was delighted. He had gotten rather bored swimming around all by himself. Doni's nostrils allowed the discharge to run off and I cleansed them daily with cotton, applying a little Vaseline to prevent them from gumming up.

Unfortunately the sinus infection became chronic, probably due to her advanced age and weakening immune system. Therefore I continued to administer antibiotics faithfully and thus was able to extend her life. It was well worth the effort. When I visited the veterinarian the next time with my greyhound his first question was: "How is Doni?" He asked how old she was and seemed amazed at her age, since normally wild ducks do not live that long. By now she was almost nine years old.

At that time I was very much aware of the fact that her days were numbered. Therefore I spent every day at least half an hour or more with her in the garden. She was most happy when sitting on my lap on the garden bench under the apple tree in the evening and would nuzzle my fingers. Sometimes she would sit on my hands. When I brought her up to my face we would look at each other lovingly and she would give me a gentle "ducky kiss" on the nose. Her feet gave away her old age and her balance was not what it used to be. Every time she tried to scratch herself she would fall over, but after all, this is also part of life; all of us are moving in the same direction, whether human or animal. Her eyes as well looked old, they were knowing eyes, tired eyes which had seen joy and sorrow.

It was my hope for her that one day she would simply fall asleep during the night and painlessly slip away. But then again I wished that day would not come too soon. I sincerely felt that we had to keep each other company for a little while longer. I needed my little duck friend as much as she needed me, maybe even more so. She was my very special companion which I could never forget. A gift from nature placed rarely in our care and I felt honored to have been chosen.

EPILOGUE FOR A PRECIOUS PET:

Last week Doni died. She had been sick for a long time, and even my daily special attention and administration of antibiotics for her by now chronic sinus infection were failing. She was in her 10th year which is ancient for a wild duck and she was loosing strength. Her balance was off, she was no longer able to care for herself and would get soaking wet whenever it rained, since she had stopped preening. What really showed her age were her eyes and feet. The eyes were tired and weepy and her feet like leather. Whenever I would administer her antibiotic I would also cover her bill with Vaseline and give her a little foot massage with it. She seemed to enjoy that part immensely. Much like an old person she had kept to herself since last summer, sitting away from her other feathered friends all by herself, snoozing away the days. Even our swimming sessions in the pool were not what they used to be. While I was all the way up to 80 laps, (in younger years she would have kept right up with me) now she would quit at 20. I would help her out of the pool, and she would sit there on the side lines contentedly watching me going back and forth.

Once, early in the fall, she seemed very bad and I called the veterinarian to inquire about the possibility of putting her to sleep. By now he knew how attached I was to my Doni and gave me a stronger antibiotic. However, last week the day I had dreaded for a long time had come. It had gotten cold early that year and she had been having trouble keeping warm. Her breathing had been labored and raspy. Lifting her I could feel the loss of muscle mass in her chest and left to her own devices she now preferred to stay in the comfort of the coop all day, sitting on the remnants of her "fuzzy" on a fresh bed of hay.

On Sunday I finally made my decision. There was no way I could watch her suffer any longer. I would rather be without her, thinking of her united with Ralph in the big blue pond beyond . So heavy-hearted and in a tearful voice I arranged for her to be put to sleep on Monday afternoon and asked the vet for a strong tranquilizer, so that she would not be afraid.

Monday morning the sun was shining, allowing her for one last time to sit in the yard which had been her home for so many years. I was supposed to administer the tranquilizer three hours prior to the vet visit. About three hours earlier I brought her into the house and let her have a last swim in the bathtub which she seemed to enjoy. Afterwards I dried her off and then, with the assistance of my husband, we sprinkled the medicine over some spaghetti, one of her favorite treats. As expected she ate every last morsel. We placed her in a cardboard box with fresh hay and her favorite fuzzy toy.

Then I sat with her in the family room stroking her head softly and talking to her, hoping she would go to sleep. To our great surprise she never did. Even after the second dose of medicine she just sat there quietly and enjoyed our attention. Eventually the time came to leave and I wrapped her in a towel, holding her tightly to my chest on the drive to the veterinarian's office. We did not talk much during the drive. Our hearts were heavy with grief over what we were about to do, knowing full well that it was the only viable option. She would no longer suffer, especially through the cold winter months.

While my husband was driving, Doni had her head firmly planted under my chin, snuggling and nuzzling me as my tears started to flow. By now she was familiar with our veterinarian who is a very gentle, caring man. He had to inject her with an anesthetic into the chest muscle, which he did while Doni was sitting on my shoulder. Then he brought in a chair for me to sit on and hold her, while the injection took effect. It happened rather quickly. One spasm and she was unconscious. I placed her gently on the table and turned my head as the veterinarian administered the final shot into the heart. I could sense the veterinarian himself was rather affected by what he had to do. After all, he had taken a special liking to the little duck with the great personality. Sadly he wrapped her up in the towel and placed her into my arms. By the time we were back in the car heading for home both my husband and I were crying. Not a word was spoken on the way back as I put my hands on the lifeless little body, feeling it getting colder and colder.

Earlier that day my husband had dug a grave for her under a very special tree, planted by my deceased father when we first moved here almost 18 years ago. We always referred to it as the Grandpa Tree and I could not think of a better resting place for her than under its branches next to the bench, where I often sit and have little heart to heart talks with my Dad. As the sun was setting we looked at her one last time, took in her special smell, kissed her head and, wrapped in the towel, gently placed her in the ground. My husband covered the hole and placed a large flat rock over her grave as a marker as well as to prevent wild animals from digging up her remains. In the spring I would plant some flowers next to it. That night we truly grieved for our special feathered friend. She had been part of the family for such a long time. Some people, and I am sure there are many, would not understand, but to us she was a gift from God, precious, trusting and utterly loving.

The children are grown now and no longer live at home. When they were told of Doni's death they were sad, since an era of their lives was over with Doni gone.

I helped her into this world, she brought me nothing but joy over her long life, she was my friend and I miss her. Having her put to sleep was one of the hardest things I ever had to do, knowing that it was in her best interest, even though I did not want to let her go. But that also is part of life.

Had she not brought me so much joy, I would not suffer the pain of loosing her so much. She will always be a most precious memory, my Doni, a duck with the mission to bring everyone whose life she touched a step closer to nature, to connect us with all living things and who gave all of herself unconditionally.

I TRULY LOVED HER!

LET'S TALK CHICKENS

One of the signs of being a true country lover is a fondness for chickens, there is no way around it. After all, what would one do without those huge brown eggs, which do not even fit into a carton for extra large store-bought ones. Traditionally chicken owners are also rather generous. They like to share their bounty with friends and neighbors.

I am presently on my fourth flock of chickens. Usually I only keep six hens which provide plenty of eggs for my friends and myself since they lay an egg each daily, unless it is very cold or they are molting.

We have established a little routine. There is a hook under my mailbox on which my friends and/or neighbors will deposit what we refer to as "chicken delight". This includes leftover vegetables, rice, noodles and other delectable treats for the hens, and when there is a need for eggs an empty egg carton will be deposited in the bag to be filled by me with fresh eggs. Not only does this help to cut down on chicken feed, it is very healthy for the birds and they in turn are the providers of huge super-colossal eggs.

My first flock of hens was hatched by a clucking chicken, which a dear friend was generous enough to let me borrow. Now that to me is a sign of true friendship, giving up even temporarily your prized clucking hen is definitely a sacrifice. She was an excellent mother hen and taught her young ones all the things a chicken needs to know, such as scratch properly, look for insects and of course how to roost, one of the more important lessons in a young chickens life. After the youngsters were old enough to fend for themselves, I returned the mother and roosters back to my friend and kept the pullets. Pretty soon it became apparent to me that, even though most people think chickens are frankly rather low on the intelligence quotient, they are actually not dumb at all, and each of them has a very distinct personality.

Naturally I named them, real good chicken names, such as Mathilda, Nelli, Henrietta, Agnes (in honor of my mother who has a good sense of humor) Wilhelmina and last but not least Psycho.

Nelli was outstanding in her affection. I used to let them roam in the yard, and if I was sitting outside relaxing for a while, she would jump in my lap and snuggle. Unfortunately she was also the first to die, but believe me, she got plenty of love while she was alive. Mathilda and Agnes were good natured and Wilhelmina was an absolute beauty, plump and dignified in the way she carried herself. Henrietta was the brightest and my protector. Yes, you guessed correctly, after all there is one in every bunch. Psycho was named for her psychotic behavior, attacking me regularly without any provocation on my part. At times she would peck my legs or feet bloody. However, all I had to do was call out: "Henrietta help" and there she was, rushing to my aid by giving Psycho a hefty peck on the head, sending her for cover. Often she would not leave my side until she was sure I had safely exited the chicken yard or coop. My family and friends thought it was hysterical and had me go into the yard for a performance of Henrietta's protective skills on purpose.

Somehow though, even though Psycho went after me with a vengeance, I never disliked her but felt empathy for her. I had observed on many occasions that she was on the very bottom of the proverbial pecking order and just could not help herself. The only way to vent her frustration was obviously to let me have it.

As I mentioned before, I am presently on my fourth flock. After the first one died I bought New Hampshire Red chicks at the local feed store and did not allow myself to get too attached, since their life span is rather short. Mine live about four to five years. Actually, I stopped naming them, however my present bunch which is three years old has two special hens reminding me of my first batch. There is "Sweet Pea", a big feathered bundle of love who likes to be picked up and cuddled, and then there is "Psycho II", you get the picture. In addition I am blessed with "Einstein", the intellectual. Right from the start "Einstein" was different. Five chicks would be in one corner of the yard and she would be off all by herself contemplating the world. Not that she is a loner, no she just seems to be a great thinker with ideas of her very own. I respect that in a chicken!

At present, since my female duck died, I have a male duck, and over the past year I believe he has notions of having become a chicken. He even insists on sleeping up with the chickens on the "poop board", and since he cannot roost, though he gave it a valiant try, I have made him a nice nest out of fresh hay in the corner. In general he gets along well with everybody.

So the next time you think "chicken", don't shortchange and dismiss them as being stupid. They are really not and each of them has a personality unlike any other. They all have different traits, personalities and temperaments. Thus they should be properly appreciated for the unique creatures they are! Our home in the country just would not be the same without them.

DON'T YOU JUST LOVE A GOOD BARTER

Bartering is sort of a lost art, although I bet in the country there is more going on than most people in suburbia or urban areas think. The other day I asked my neighbor down the street if he needed some of my super-colossal eggs which I am blessed with, and he gratefully accepted a carton (held together by a rubber band since it will not close otherwise due to the size of the eggs), but in exchange he offered me three heads of lettuce, three cucumbers, three eggplants and three peppers from his fall garden. What a treasure! After I returned home I realized that there was no way, being empty nesters, my husband and I could enjoy all this bounty. So I called my neighbors on the other side. They are a retired couple in their 80ies and I offered them some fresh veggies. I gave them a head of lettuce, one large cucumber, one eggplant and two peppers (I am not that fond of peppers, they don't agree with me). As luck would have it, they had just received a large carton of peaches from a visiting relative and were all too happy to load me up with fresh peaches.

Now my carton of super-colossal eggs had provided me with two heads of lettuce, one pepper, two cucumbers, two eggplants and a whole bunch of fresh, deliciously juicy peaches. What a deal!

The entire matter came full circle when I took the leftover vegetable scraps such as lettuce leaves, peelings from the cucumbers and eggplants as well as peaches out to the chicken yard, where they were a more than welcome addition to the regular chicken feed. Now I will be blessed again with huge fresh eggs and so will my neighbors. Bartering is one of those odd things us country folks truly enjoy, even in the last rural corner of the nations most populated State - New Jersey.

SNOWDROPS

AS FAR BACK AS I REMEMBER I HAVE DELIGHTED IN YOUR APPEARANCE. YOU HAVE SHOWN UP ALWAYS WHEN I NEEDED YOU. HUMBLE IN YOUR PLAIN WHITE GARMENT BUT ALSO STUNNING IN YOUR EXQUISITE BEAUTY.

WHEN I WAS LITTLE I WOULD LOOK FOR YOU, THE FIRST SIGN OF SPRING, AND SURE ENOUGH, THERE YOU WERE, FAITHFULLY ANNOUNCING THAT SPRING WAS NOT TOO FAR AHEAD. YES THERE WERE TIMES I HAD TO SEARCH FOR YOU IN THE SNOW, BUT YOU ALWAYS FOUND A LITTLE CORNER OF SUNSHINE WHERE YOU MADE YOUR FIRST APPEARANCE, AND I WOULD LITERALLY JUMP FOR JOY!

NOW I KNOW EXACTLY WHERE TO FIND YOU, SINCE I PLANTED YOU, WHOSE LITTLE BULBS COME FROM ANOTHER WORLD, WHERE MY MOTHER DUG THEM FROM HER GARDEN, AND I PLANTED YOU WITH LOVE IN FRONT OF THE GREENHOUSE BY A SHRUB. THERE, NOW ONCE AGAIN YOU STAND, AND SHOW YOURSELF WITH CHARM, HUMILITY AND GRACE. WHAT A GOOD FRIEND YOU ARE. I KNOW OF NONE I CAN RELY ON MORE.

YOUR WHITE DRESS IS STUNNING AND PICKING UP YOUR LITTLE HEAD I SEE THE DAINTY CENTER RIMMED IN PROMISING GREEN. YOUR PROMISE IS TRUE ALWAYS. SOMETIMES YOU ARE SURPRISED AND COVERED UNDER A WHITE BLANKET OF LATE SNOW. BUT YOU ARE A SURVIVOR AND SIMPLY DRAW BACK INTO THE EARTH FROM WHERE YOU CAME, PATIENTLY WAITING FOR ANOTHER SUNSHINE. ONE THAT WILL LAST AND ALLOW YOU TO SHOUT "SPRING" TO ALL THOSE WHO HAVE THE EAR TO LISTEN.

TRULY, YOU ARE MY FAVORITE AMONG THE MULTITUDE OF SPRING FLOWERS, FOR I RESPECT YOUR PERSISTENCE, RELIABILITY AND BEAUTY. TODAY YOU TOLD ME NOT IN WORDS, BUT BY SIMPLY BEING THERE, THAT ONCE AGAIN SPRING IS JUST AROUND THE CORNER, AND I JUMP FOR JOY!

BIRD CRAZY

Did you ever hold a wild bird in your hands? No, not one that was injured and you tried to help, but one that came to your outstretched hand filled with birdseed voluntarily, sat down with perfect ease, and of it's own free will stayed awhile, taking it's time to pick out just the right morsel to eat?

I have had the privilege many times. It takes a certain amount of patience. I truly believe the inherent love for any living creature comes across and allows the animal to trust me.

I don't really know exactly when I became "bird crazy" (I spend more money on birdseed than clothing for myself over the course of a year), but it goes way back into my childhood. My mother had a wonderful story, which I asked her to tell me over and over again, as little children will do. When she had been a little girl like me, this was prior to World War I, her family had lived in a Brownstone in Cologne, Germany. They had a little backyard, where one day her mother, my much beloved Oma, had found two chickadee fledglings. Apparently their mother had perished and so they had taken the birds in, hand-fed them with bread and insects and eventually were ready to release them. Only they had never left. In those days there were no screen windows during the summer. One just opened the windows for fresh air and the birds would fly in and out of the house whenever they pleased. They would perch on my mother's shoulders or hands, sometimes land on her head, and when my grandfather returned from work for his supper, they would sit at the edge of his plate and wait patiently for him to share a little food with them. This wonderful event had lasted all summer, until one day, Haenschen and Peterchen, as they were called, could not be found. My mother searched the backyard diligently and eventually found some feathers and little black feet. The neighbor's cat had caught them. Naturally my mother had been inconsolable and from that point on hated cats as much as she loved birds. When I was little this story had all the impact of a great drama on me and created an interest in birds at a very early age.

Actually my first pet, I must have been about 3 years old, was a Bantam chicken following me everywhere, was housetrained and even took naps with me. Unfortunately I had a similar experience as my mother, since one day it simply disappeared and was found years later, flat as a pancake and mummified, behind the potato crate in the old basement. Apparently it had slipped behind and could not get out. I cried for a long time and missed my pet immensely.

Nevertheless, the hook to become a true bird lover had been set and not all of my experiences had an unhappy ending. As a matter of fact, my love for birds has greatly enhanced my life over the past 50 years.

There was the time one fall, when I found an injured European robin redbreast, which could not possibly migrate south. I took it to my mother who fashioned a little splint for its broken leg, and we kept it with ample food and water in the basement of our new house, where it could move about freely. It was not a dingy basement and had a number of windows, so every day after school I would go down there and visit my little feathered friend.

In time he began to trust me, and I could entice him to perch on my finger. Eventually he wood take food from my hand and our friendship blossomed. That Christmas became very special to us all, since my father, who likewise was an animal lover, suggested we allow the bird, which was well by now, to come upstairs and sit in the Christmas tree. I can still see it in my mind and hear the joyous song when it spotted the tree. Perched on its top branches he simply sang his heart out. I think it was my best Christmas ever!

Spring arrived and my mother told me that now the time had come to let the bird go. I was devastated. I had gotten so attached to it, but she explained to me that when you really love a wild animal, you have to give it the freedom it was given by it's maker, and so with a heavy heart I took my little friend outside into the backyard and let him go. He hung around for a few days, but it was spring, breeding season, and so one day he followed his instinct and we no longer saw him. You can well imagine that he still lives very much in my heart, even after all these years.

When I became a teenager and during the early years of my marriage, by now I had made a new home in the United States, the "affliction" somewhat abated, like a disease which goes away for a while and then resurfaces with a vengeance. After my oldest son was born and we bought a home in the northwestern part of New Jersey, the bird feeders went up during the first winter. I could not believe my eyes when I spotted the first cardinal and blue jay, birds which are not native to Germany. My son and I would watch the comings and goings for long periods of time, since one bird feeder was suspended from a hemlock branch right in front of his bedroom window. So he got his training early. I am proud to say, that even while in College, he asked me which birdseed to buy, since he had attached a birdfeeder to his dorm window. Now, at 25 and living on his own in an apartment, there are several feeders on his balcony. Much like myself, he has fallen victim to this strange condition of " bird craziness". He tells me, that he finds bird watching enormously stress relieving and I fully agree!

Once we moved to our present home, which is located further out in northwestern New Jersey on 5 acres, things became really serious. By now I had two boys, who delighted in building whimsical and odd bird feeders and houses which dot the property. Over the past 18 years our place has become a virtual bird sanctuary. Early in the spring the bird houses are cleaned for their new occupants and are filled in no time at all. We must have raised literally hundreds of birds over the years and I have taken to feeding year-round (that's why my birdseed budget exceeds my clothing expenses). But it is well worth it. The bird identification book, which I acquired many years ago, is always handy to identify someone who is new to me. Just last week I had the privilege to observe a male and female cardinal on the same branch as an indigo bunting, a truly spectacular sight!

My younger son likewise grew up to be a bird enthusiast, and there is nothing which makes my heart joyous and tells me I have done well as a mother, than seeing him, who is in College now, come home for his winter break and patiently stand outside in the snow-covered yard, holding up his hand with black oil sunflower seed. Just watching the expression on his face when a bird fearlessly lands on his hand is wonderful. His smile indicates pure joy and he has brought in many a bird which flew against a window and lay stunned on the ground. Mostly together we were able to revive them and release them as soon as they had recovered. Sometimes it takes just a little tender holding and loving to get them over the shock. At other times an overnight stay maybe required. However mostly, unless they suffered a broken neck (and that makes us very sad), we are able to rescue them. To minimize these occurrences I have placed flower stickers on the inside of the windows of the house, so they can see the obstacle in their way.

Over the years some things have changed. They are to me a clear indication of climate changes, such as for instance this year the rose breasted grosbeak are staying, while in the past they would have simply recharged their batteries in my yard and then headed on to New England. Also we have experienced some rather strange winters lately. Sometimes the robins did not migrate at all but stuck around all year.

Due to my passion for birds I have become a pretty good weather forecaster. I know when a storm is approaching, be it a blizzard or a summer storm, mostly way ahead before the professionals on TV. I can tell when winter or spring will start by watching for the Canadian geese which migrate right over my house. As luck would have it, we seem to have built our house right under the main flight path. Usually, sometime during the first week of October, I will hear in the distance a familiar honking, and after looking around and waiting for a while, the well known V formation of these magnificent animals will fly right overhead due south. Depending on the jet stream the migration will continue with flock after flock moving through for days. Then I know that 6 weeks later the cold weather can be expected. The same scenario will repeat itself in the northern direction in late March. The birds are always correct, and I have learned to distinguish by now between the "locals" and the ones which are on their way to distant places. I always wish them well on their journey, and there are times I would just love to travel with them. Another wonderful indicator of the changing seasons is the first sighting of the blue heron. They always make me think of prehistoric birds, a leftover from a time when the earth was young. The gathering of the starlings in the fall is likewise a phenomenon, which I enjoy immensely. They will appear in never ending waves, dipping and rising in an ancient dance. I always marvel that there never seems to be a collision, even though they fly so closely together. If only people could behave like that on the highways. There seems to be no "road rage" among our feathered friends.

But let me get back to some of the more intimate encounters I have had along the way, the ones which are just edged in my mind and heart because somehow I was able to give something back to the creatures, which have nurtured my soul for so long.

There was for instance the pigeon, which one morning, when I was driving my oldest son to school, was sitting in the middle of the road. He made no effort to get out of the way, so I stopped and got out of the car. He allowed me to pick him up without fear.

There did not seem to be any injury, he was just exhausted and he must have belonged to someone since he wore a band around his leg.

After dropping my son off at school I drove home with the bird sitting quietly on my lap and I placed him in a good-sized cardboard box with food and water. He ate and drank heartily, then fell into a deep sleep. Hours later, when he awoke, I could pick him up, and he would perch on my finger checking me out curiously. There was no fear. He was definitely a tame bird. Thinking he was well and recovered I took him outside to send him on his way, but he had no intention of leaving. He stayed with us for a week, eating, drinking and sleeping. Then one day, when I tried to give him his freedom again, he took wing, circled over the house three times to orient himself and flew off with my blessings.

My family will never forget that incidence nor will they forget the time a grackle fell down the chimney of our antique wood-burning kitchen stove (which thank God was not in use at the time),and was unable to free himself. We could hear him struggle inside and after thinking what to do, one of us came up with a brilliant idea. We removed the bottom tray which allows access to the ashes that accumulate around the baking oven. It worked! The bird spotted a ray of light and escaped through the little opening. He was blacker than black, covered with soot and leaving marks all over our kitchen. Eventually we were able to get him into the family room and catch him, but not before he met up with our little parakeet named Ignatius, or Iggi for short, who spends most of his time outside his cage on a perch near the window. The two of them were terrified and I finally found them, funny enough huddled in the same corner just inches away from each other, making noises of utmost distress. It was almost a human cry for help. After that experience I doubt very much the grackle ever ventured down our chimney pipe again.

My last remarks will be devoted to the tiniest of our feathered friends, the humming bird. Naturally, and how could you think otherwise, there is a humming bird feeder hanging from a tree branch next to the deck, where in the evening hours we can watch them coming and going to stock up for the night. They are the ruby-throated kind, and often we have observed battles over territory or eligible females during breeding season. Knowing now that we will not harm them, they have become very tame, and I have stood next to the feeder with a humming bird hovering in front of my face almost touching my nose. Once, on a Sunday morning, I was reading the New York Times, when I heard the familiar humming nearby. As I slowly lowered the paper he was right on the other side. I truly did not know humming birds could read!

Yes, I admit to being "Bird Crazy" but since there are worse things to catch in this world I grin and bear my fate. It has enriched my life in so many ways and I would not change this strange affliction for anything in the world.

THE DOVES ARE BACK

Our doves are back, in the very same spot they nested last year, namely on top of the wooden fence which encloses our small "secret garden". Last year they were more visible but the honeysuckle climbing the fence has spread considerably since, and once we spotted them feeding in the "secret garden", we had an inkling that they had returned to last year's home.

Indeed, a few days later I gently moved aside a few branches and there she was, sitting on her nest of small twigs and looking at me with trusting eyes, knowing well I would not hurt or disturb her.

My husband and I remember our resident doves fondly from last year, when they hatched not one but two broods, and we were privileged to watch the entire process. They made a good team, never leaving the nest alone, which was a good thing because the other end of the fence was occupied by our resident garter snake and a favorite spot for her on sunny days. Surely it had crossed her mind that not too far from her there were tasty eggs or young birds, but the parents keep a tight watch and so they coexisted peacefully. Nevertheless I worried!

Our doves are mourning doves which, I understand, have a rather short life span. Maybe that is why they raised two broods. There is something very special about the trust of a wild animal that does not even blink an eye when you walk by, work in the garden or have dinner outside. They went about their business and we about ours. Last year I felt sorry for them since they got soaking wet whenever it rained, but this year the increased foliage from the honeysuckle grants more protection from the elements. Hopefully the couple will again be successful in raising their young, while we can watch the rapid process of their growing up. We were astounded how little time it took for them to go from the baby bird to the fledgling stage. Of course our camera was out of film when one Sunday afternoon we looked out into the "secret garden" and there, right on the gate leading to the driveway, were Mama Dove and Papa Dove with their two young ones in between, getting their first flying lessons. As is common in all families, siblings are not all alike, and one was more daring and adept at the new skill than the other. It took off for short distances and returned with a smooth, safe landing while the other one had to be coaxed into leaving the safety of the wooden gate. Once in the air it fluttered about for a short while until it seemed to get the hang of it, and then landed rather wobbly back on the fence facing the wrong way. As far as we could tell, the parents were rather encouraging and patient, for about an hour later both fledglings were equally adept at taking off, flying and landing safely. While they did return to the nest for a little time longer, a couple of weeks later we no longer saw them but to our great surprise Mama and Papa mourning dove had started a new family and were back on the nest to follow nature's call.

It was great to be able to enjoy the process twice in one season and so you can imagine how thrilled we were this spring, when we discovered they were back. So is the garter snake but this year we will not worry. We know the doves are always prepared to watch out for their family and now we wait (with camera loaded nearby) for the next generation to take wing. Who knows, maybe they make the top of the fence around the "secret garden" the ancestral homestead, and we will be blessed year after year with their much cherished presence. They are certainly welcome!

P.S. Looking out of our window during the first snowfall in December I saw 8 mourning doves perched in a row on top of the fence where they nested. Somehow I had the feeling I was looking at several generations having a family gathering.

IN DEFENSE OF THE DANDELION

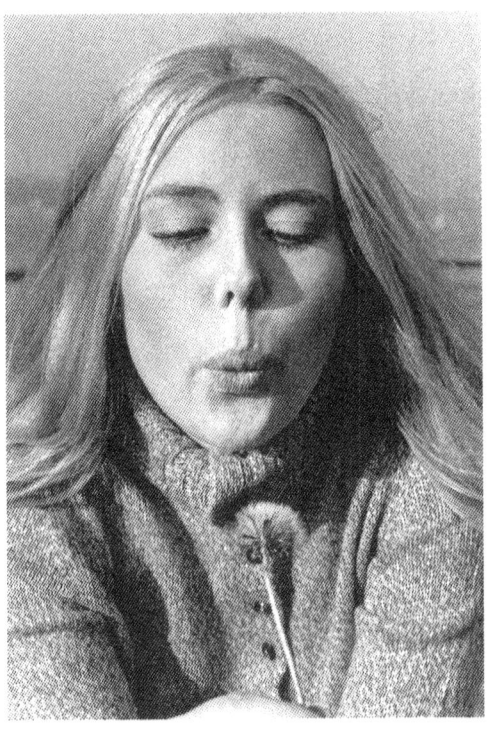

As funny as it may sound and being sort of a country gal, to me people fall into two categories. Those who absolutely must have an English turf lawn, the perfection of a green surface looking like "Astroturf" and those who can sit back, look out onto their front lawn and relish the appearance of dandelions, crabgrass and other wild, naturally growing plants which are green. Of course I fall into the latter category for the following simple reasons: The "Astroturf" lawn lover's lawn tells me something about the personality, namely he or she is the extremely fastidious type, uptight and not laid back at all. Just the mere appearance of a lone dandelion having invaded his pride and joy can drive him into a frenzy and cause him to bite his nails to the quick. It also separates him from the true country lover and reveals his desire to keep up with the Jonses: my lawn is greener than yours. Not to mention the amount of fertilizer, pesticides, herbicides and use of precious water during dry spells, none of which are good for our environment.

The true country lover like myself delights in the fact that the lawn is natural, admires the yellow flowers of the dandelions, uses their fresh leaves in salads and, once the dandelions have gone to seed, enjoys watching the finches feed on them. The lawn is a haven for wildlife. "Martha" the groundhog comes out every night to graze, rabbits frolic about in the most hilarious manner, and I have observed them performing incredible acrobatic feats. Deer come and lay down right in front of my house without fear, sometimes I feel I live in "Disney Land" since Bambi shows up.

Once the dandelion season is over, and it only lasts a few weeks briefly reappearing in the fall, my lawn is just as green if not greener than anybody's, requires minimum care and remains a haven for wildlife during the entire summer months for me to enjoy.

Actually, when a dry spell hits, my lawn is the greenest around, since the natural groundcover withstands such periods with ease, while the "Astroturf" lawn turns brown and ugly. I save the cost of fertilizer, pesticides and herbicides, thus not contributing to the pollution of groundwater or the demise of precious songbirds. My yard is alive, a natural playground for anything from butterflies to wild turkeys, no less in New Jersey, the most densely populated state of the nation.

This is how I like it, and the older and wiser I get, the more I enjoy the serenity I derive, from what reminds me of the meadows surrounding the home so far away where I grew up.

For those who despise the look, beware, dandelions are devious and spiteful to people they know don't care for them. Should you fall under the first mentioned category, and this is not a judgement call reflecting on your character in any negative fashion whatsoever, let me fill you in on a few challenges when dealing with dandelions. First of all, simply upon hearing the noise of an approaching lawn mower they will lay down flat hugging the ground, which I believe to be a natural defense mechanism on their part, only to stand up again in their full glory as soon as you have completed your mowing and feel totally satisfied with the result. This may add unnecessary stress to an already stressed-out personality type. Furthermore, watch out for people like myself, who delight in picking a dandelion once it has gone to seed, blow on it and thus allow the seeds to take wing, possibly spreading to your "Astroturf". Since this is still a free country and since our legislators have not yet found a way to outlaw the spreading of dandelion seed, you are in big trouble and your only alternative maybe to move your lawn. I am staying put!

Should you try and manually root out the dandelion, be aware that it grows a deep tap root, which, rumor has it, sometimes goes all the way to China. Here again you are faced with a major problem: either end up with painful back spasms sending you to the nearest Chiropractor or resort to a potent herbicide, which sooner or later will make its way into the ground water and might hasten your own demise. As the above shows, it is very clear that the dandelion has the upper hand! It has been here for a lot longer than we have and will be here long after we are gone.

So why be obsessed with rooting out a beautiful flower which God put on this earth to delight the senses and feed his creatures.

When my children were little, one Mother's Day my then 4 year old son happily presented me with a big bouquet of dandelions. It still stands out in my mind as one of the sweetest things he ever did for me and 23 years later the memory of that magic moment can put a smile on my face. Yes, I openly admit to being a nonconformist in many ways, but that is what makes life interesting. LET'S HEAR IT FOR THE DANDELION!

THE "OPA" TREE

By Inge Perreault

My father had this special love of trees, I always knew that. Right after the war, he purchased a sizeable piece of property in the country on the outskirts of Cologne, Germany, where he planted every conceivable kind of fruit tree he could think of. So as a child I tasted them all. In June I stuffed my mouth with sweet or sour cherries, worked myself through different kinds of plums as well as apples and pears until finally, at the very end of the season, Father would pick the first Ontario apple.

With great care he selected his choice and presented it to us at dinner. A "Poem" of a fruit he would exclaim, after admiring its beauty and then cut it up carefully into slices for all of us to taste. This was an annual family ritual. The rest of the Ontario apples would go into storage, keeping us in apples for most of the winter.

My Father loved all kinds of trees, but his favorite was the German oak. Whenever we would come across a fallen oak tree on our traditional Sunday afternoon walks during my childhood, he would make it a point to stop and explain to me in great detail what you could tell from the insides of a tree. You could count the rings and find out the age, even determine whether it had been a dry or a wet season by their size. He truly instilled in me a reverence for trees and one of my still unfulfilled wishes is to hug a Redwood sometime in the future.

I learned early how to distinguish all the trees in the forest by their leaves, bark or fruit. The prankster came out in him when I was little. By making me look up into a big fir tree heavy with snow, then quickly shaking it, I would stand there all covered in white flakes. He used to laugh so heartily that I indulged him in this game for a long time, long after I had caught on what he was up to. His glee was so great at having gotten the better of me once more, it was worth getting some snow melting down my neck. I could see a glimpse of what he must have been like as a little boy.

In 1980, on one of my father's visits with my family in this country, he planted a Norway maple sapling on our 5 acres in northern New Jersey, where my husband and I planned to build our dream house. From the day he planted it, we've always referred to this tree as the Opa Tree (German for Grandpa). We have pictures of my two boys being small, standing beside it being the same height. But as the years went by he would frequently ask in letters or on the telephone about the progress and well-being of his tree and we in turn would send back pictures, usually flanked by his grandsons. Pretty soon the Opa Tree dwarfed my sons and it has grown into a magnificent specimen of its kind with a sturdy healthy trunk and a wonderful symmetrical shape. By now it is about 30 feet tall and turns the most spectacular yellow late in the fall. It is always the last tree to shed its leaves.

The spring he died I was there on a visit for what were to be his last 12 days. An old college pal was to pick me up at the airport, and I truly had not expected to see my father due to his advanced age. However, there he was, dressed in his finest to welcome me. Right then and there I knew by the pallor in his face that he did not have much time left. His heart was giving out.

Strangely enough, his favorite Ontario apple tree, planted almost 45 years earlier, was dying too. It was understood and accepted that we would most likely see each other for the last time. It was so very difficult for both of us. Especially now, that we had finally found common ground after years of conflict and really gotten to like each other. The fact that he was 82 with a full life behind him did not make it any easier. Many times, during those last 12 days, I would find him standing all by himself under the Ontario apple tree, carefully checking for sings of life since it was early spring. He looked very forlorn and when I asked what he was thinking, he would get a far away look in his tired eyes and answer: " Well Inge, everything has to come to an end sometime."

He was right! He waited until I left, virtually willing himself to live in order to spare me the pain and had his heart attack while I was crossing the Atlantic back to the United States. I shall never forget the moment when I looked back from my friend's car at my father and our eyes locked, saying our final good-byes.

When I got home from visiting my elderly parents and found out he had passed away, I fell ill and was in no shape to turn right around, fly back and attend the funeral. I was physically and emotionally spent and so my eldest son represented the family. Guess what, Opa found his final resting place under a German oak.

The day of the funeral my husband, myself and our younger son had our very own ceremony and closure in our own special way. While the actual funeral was taking place thousands of miles away, we attached a beautiful huge ribbon to the trunk of the tree. We all stood underneath its branches and I read the chapter on "Death" from the Prophet by Kahlil Gibran. To those of you who are familiar with its message, it is very powerful, yet positive.

Since then the Opa Tree gets a special ribbon for each season, white for Easter, rust in the fall, red for Christmas and golden for his birthday. There is a bench under it on which all of us like to sit and reflect. I have my little heart to heart talks with my father in joyous and in painful times where I can feel him speaking to me directly through the rustling leaves. "Don't worry," I hear him say, "it will all work out and never forget that after each storm the sun will come out again, count on that!" It will forever be the Opa Tree, special to us all.

I returned to Germany the following spring and stood at my father's grave site. Though I knew his earthly remains were resting there, I could not feel his presence – not the way I feel it while sitting under the Opa Tree. In my heart, the Opa Tree is where his spirit dwells.

THE ILLUSIVE EASTER BUNNY

Easter seemed to arrive earlier when I was a very little girl back in Germany. Since the climate is milder in the Rhineland, the Easter Bunny's gifts were usually to be found among crocuses, daffodils and tulips in the garden, as well as on our customary walks through the woods taking place on Easter Sunday afternoons.

I would run outside in my nightgown early in the morning and find little nests of colorful eggs here and there amongst the early spring flowers, placing them carefully into my Easter basket. Sometimes I had to search really hard to find them tucked away under leaves or under shrubs around the house. Once all the treasures were found in our yard, some of the Easter eggs would be eaten for breakfast and then we would get ready for Easter Service, which to a little girl of 3 or 4 seemed to last an eternity.

After a sumptuous big meal, in Germany the main meal is served at lunch time, I had to take a nap. Then the entire family would go for the traditional afternoon walk in the woods. I was the youngest member, born just after World War II, and my sisters were 9 and 12 years older than me.

My grandparents, already way into their 80ies, took special joy in surprising me with little treats along the path we would take through the woods that day. I remember well how exciting and amazing this was to me and just how cunning I thought the Easter Bunny was. He seemed to know exactly which path we would take for a stroll that afternoon and leave his colorful eggs or chocolate bunnies, wrapped in bright shiny foil, just where I could find them.

It took me a few more year to find out, that Grandpa had taken the very same path during my naptime and taken over the serious duties of the Easter Bunny, hiding treats in mossy greens, by the roots of trees and under rocks by the little stream along the path. The trees were just starting to send out their first buds. These are memories of my childhood which make up a little for all the hardship I experienced during the immediate post-war years, such as growing up in a three room wooden shack without running water, electricity and of course with an outhouse. After all, Germany lay in ruins, but to a little girl Easter surprises like the ones I had, made up for all the things today's children take so much for granted.

Those memories are still very special to me. Once I had children here in the United States, I tried my very best to create Easter surprises for my two young sons, similar to the ones I used to treasure so much during my own childhood.

My parents were very supportive in this effort and would send Easter packages, containing some of the German Easter favorites for their grandchildren.

Whenever the weather permitted, I would make it a point to get up very early in the morning and, carrying our Easter goodies in a large basket, make my way down to the woods of our property. There, along the path leading to the creek, I looked for proper hiding places which I found under leaves of budding skunk cabbage, in mossy areas by the trunks of our large oak trees and even in hollowed out branches the winter storms had broken off the trees. Not only did it bring back wonderful memories, I really had fun playing the ILLUSIVE EASTER BUNNY, which cunningly hid colorful eggs and other treasurers in the most unlikely places. There was always the chance that prior to our arrival later, some of the "goodies" might be found and eaten by wildlife. However, during all the years when our children were little this never happened once, a fact that amazes me to this day.

I can still see my little boys, (who are now young men towering over me) jump out of bed and get dressed in record speed, grab their Easter baskets and head outside, running as fast as their little legs would carry them down to the woods. My husband and I followed them slowly, happily listening to their shouting: "look what I found" or "I cannot believe the Easter Bunny knew about this special knot hole in our favorite tree!" They would search diligently and eventually follow the path along the softly gurgling creek, finding little nests of Easter surprises here and there, until their baskets were full to the brim.

In their minds, like in mine when I was little, this was a terribly exciting search. Today they look back rather fondly to these special times, when the Easter Bunny came and found the best hiding places in the woods. However, this was usually not the only surprise, because strange as it may seem, every year we would come across the first pair of Mallard ducks swimming merrily down the stream.

This too was something wonderful to observe and became part of our Easter experiences. Having found the gifts the Easter Bunny left behind, we would slowly walk back to the house and prepare a delicious breakfast with some of the colorful eggs. Then we would all get dressed in our Sunday outfits, go to Church and celebrate the true meaning of Easter Sunday. I bet that to my boys the Easter Service likewise seemed to last an eternity, at least until they were old enough to understand, that Easter signified a lot more than the illusive Easter Bunny hiding treasures in the woods.

A MOTHER'S HEART – A SECRET GARDEN

A mother's heart resembles a small enchanted garden, surrounded by a fence which contains and protects everything therein. In the spring the dogwood and the little corkscrew weeping birch which overshadows the waterfall reveal their first signs of life. The little snowdrops virtually jump out of the ground near the stone surround of the pool into which the waterfall empties, and the fiddle head ferns, taken from the woods, work their way upwards and begin to unfold like magic. Likewise the may apples and jack-in- the- pulpit make their first appearance. The crocuses are long gone by now, and you have to burn their image into your mind since, like with a baby, the changes taking place from day to day, occur so very quickly. Next the daffodils show up and the astilbe carefully peek out, sending their first shoots above ground. Like the baby which now fills out physically and recognizes his parents, the child develops his first character traits which will remain in place for the rest of a lifetime.

The colorful tulips and azaleas, short-lived but spectacular in their color, follow in rapid succession and suddenly the child is no longer a baby but a developing little human being with his very own likes and dislikes. He discovers that there is a big world out there to be explored and on which he can exert an influence, the significance of which will remain a mystery yet for years to come. The heart of the mother absorbs all this and cherishes the moments, but also feels at times like the little Cherub in the secret garden who, so it seems, carries the entire

mass of honeysuckle on it's little shoulders. But that is only an illusion, for in reality a higher power is at work here, and the root of the honeysuckle is firmly anchored in the earth from which it grew.

Time passes and the trees are now covered in fresh green foliage. The water splashes joyfully from the top rock of the waterfall, cascading down into the little pond where birds as well as chipmunks come to drink or bathe. The spring flowers are merely a distant memory and the child now goes to school. For the first time the mother's heart feels a stab of pain, the pain of separation and a distancing, for different individuals now exercise an influence on the child one has had all to oneself.

It hurts the heart a little because she is not needed quite as much. However, she now has a little time to herself and other pursuits, which is not a bad thing.

The mother plants her annuals in the little garden to give it color, knowing full well they will not return the following year. Summer arrives and passes in a flash or so it seems. Likewise the school years pass too quickly with the great multitude of activities. Then, suddenly, there is a teenager sitting at the dinner table and everything changes once again. It is a constant coming and going and adjusting to new circumstances. Sometimes it is uncomfortably hot and she withdraws into the shade, likewise at times the mother is confronted with heated arguments, because the child has now formed his own opinions and is no longer willing to be guided easily. So the mother leaves things be and thinks to herself: "just wait", for she remembers her very own years of rebellion and knows exactly where the real dangers lurk.

If confronted with those she will speak out forcefully. She wants to continue protecting her child at all cost but she meets limits. A further stab in the heart is felt, and this one becomes almost overwhelming, when autumn arrives in the secret garden and the child, now a young adult, leaves home for college. He is away alone for the first time and totally dependent on himself. The mother finds herself drifting during the course of the day into the child's room and sits down on the bed, where so many times stories were read, sickness was nursed and care was taken that physically and emotionally everything was in good order. Here she sits, all alone, for even to the heart of a father these feelings in a mother's heart are an enigma. She sheds some tears, buries her face into his pillow in order to recall the familiar smell of this child whom she loves so deeply. Where did the time go? Just yesterday, she thinks, I was a young woman and now I see the first wrinkles and gray hair when looking in the mirror. With a deep sigh she leaves the child's room and goes into the garden, where she reflects on these momentous changes. There the recognition comes, that likewise the garden has entered a new phase. The leaves on the trees have turned color, not unlike her hair and the ferns look a little tattered and worn. The splendor of spring and summer are gone, there is no turning back! She tries to shield the annuals, which were planted in late spring, by covering them from an early frost in order to hold on to them, just like she calls the young student much too frequently inquiring if all is well. The instinct of a mother is not easily extinguished. The urge to protect as long as possible is hard to yield. However, one night the strong frost comes and in the morning the flowers lie flat and lifeless on the ground. The young man, who was birthed under great pain and whom she raised with love, patience and much effort, meets his first difficulties and disappointments of the heart. The mother understands all too well and listens, attempts to point out the correct path and soothe the pain but ultimately leaves his actions up to his own judgement. After all, he will experience many difficulties in his life and will have to get used to dealing with them on his own, without allowing them to destroy him. She knows from her own experience how hard life can be; how unfair and how very unpredictable at times.

But she does not want to rob him of his innocence and idealism, not yet and not by me, she thinks. Leave him a while longer with the illusion that indeed life is fair and just. Was it not painful enough for her to come to the conclusion that this is not so?

Slowly and unavoidably winter approaches. The secret garden, the reservoir of the mother's soul, lies dormant. Much like the birds which come to feed within the protected enclosure, the son returns from time to time. He enjoys his favorite meals, telling the mother what he wants her to know but never more. Yet the feeling cannot be denied; he does not live here any longer! Yes, he will always live in the mother's heart, until she takes her last breath, but the separation has almost been completed. He receives his degree, enters the workforce and moves into his own apartment.

The first snow transforms the garden into a winter paradise. It is beautiful but getting colder. Again the heart of the mother experiences the by now familiar ache. For the holidays small white lights decorate the trees and look lovely. The son gets engaged and another woman takes the place of the mother, which she has held so long with steadfast love and great devotion. Now she must move aside and let go. Twenty five years are a long time. Will it take another twenty five years until the pain subsides? She thinks not, for life has to go on. After all, she was only the medium through with the Almighty continued his great plan. Her own world takes on a new dimension and it is time to concentrate on herself. To heck with wrinkles and gray hair, to heck with physical infirmities and limitations which are beginning to emerge, and most of all to heck with self-pity. The mother's own personality must continue to unfold and stretch once more into new directions. The garden waits patiently for the next spring, when it once more awakens and becomes life affirming.

At some time in the future the mother will sit there with a grandchild on her knees whom she will read favorite stories to. The circle will have closed entirely and this is the way it must be.

The heart of a mother knows no boundaries and it embraces all experiences, good as well as bad, with love. Now she is no longer needed but though this is the way of the world, the recognition is not an easy one to digest. There is only one thing to do. To make the best of all that occurs and quietly watch from the sidelines when the son goes through his own joys, trials and tribulations. To be there selflessly and ready to give advice when asked for. Otherwise to stand back and turn to her very own purpose in life, to find fulfillment in the knowledge that, while she has some influence and is much loved, ultimately one can only count on oneself. Yes, the heart of a mother is a wondrous and mysterious place during all seasons indeed. The secret and enchanted garden grew out of this heart in more ways than words can tell. Perhaps unconditional love is the only expression which comes to mind and does it justice.

CHILDREN AND PETS –
A GROWTH EXPERIENCE FOR MOM

There is a part to raising children in the country which involves animals and their care. Now it is true that this applies to a large extend to parental experience in general. However, for those of you who live in the country, this takes on larger dimensions than for instance the family raising children in an urban environment. It seems to me the animals are more numerous and varied.

There are times a mother is confronted with species she is not necessarily fond of or wants to share her home with.

After having raised two active boys who are now adults, I can look back with a certain sense of humor and compassion for young parents who are faced with the tasks of children and pet care. This is an aspect of parenthood they probably never gave much thought to, however it is one not to be taken lightly.

Sometime in between having a toddler and a college student at home, you will be making certain experiences which will parallel mine! In order to explain the scope of this entire matter I should probably start from the very beginning and take you back to the first pet in my home, followed by years of dealing with different species. One day, my older son must have been about 2, I was introduced to "Snooky", a black and white stray cat who decided to be his buddy and swiftly moved in. Now it is difficult to expect a 2 year old to feed a cat and clean a litter box, but I tried to explain future responsibilities, foolishly hoping to plant the seed. Snooky was a good cat, as cats go. Naturally she had to get shots and be neutered by a vet who made a pass at me, (I was much younger then) and also brought fleas into the house not once but twice, who bit no one else but me, eventually requiring the services of an exterminator at considerable cost. My advice to young parents: "Take the money and put it in a College Fund instead." After Snooky, who disappeared one day as mysteriously as she had entered our lives, there was Agnes, a cute tabby. I had changed vets by then who did not make passes.

This was followed by my son's intense desire to call a fish tank his own. Now I was sure I had hit the jackpot. A 5 year old is surely capable of feeding fish. Meanwhile I was busy with another baby, but alas, had it not been for my tender care, compassion and good nature, the fish would surely have perished. As it turned out, the fish tank episode lasted only two years, then we got into delightful creatures such as geckos and other lizards. Mind you, I am not a friend of slimy crawling things, but on the other hand I am a great animal lover and so once again I gave in. Of course you do not have to ask who ended up cleaning the terrarium and feeding icky worms, stored in my refrigerator, to the lizards. I held lectures which fell on deaf ears and time passed. Then one day they staged the big escape, just prior to our leaving for a 3 week trip to Europe, and I thought: "What the heck, let them fend for themselves!" Upon our return one morning my husband started making funny noises while taking his shower, and when I checked further into these strange sounds, I found out where the geckos were. They were stuck to the inside of the shower curtain and very much alive!!!

The following year we made the move to our house further out into the countryside, where on 5 acres of fields, woods and a stream, we built the passive solar dream house we had designed ourselves. Sometime during that move we lost Agnes. She disappeared into the woods never to be seen again.

Living in a rather remote area of course one absolutely must have a dog, preferably a large one if one's husband travels a lot. Enthusiastically we decided on a good watchdog and purchased a Dalmation puppy. The boys, now 8 and 4 years old, promised faithfully to take the dog out and walk him daily. The novelty of that wore off quickly. They were always busy with other pressing things to do, and so once again dear old Mom was stuck with feeding the dog and walking him. Grudgingly I told myself that this was good exercise, and I really started to enjoy it. Smoke was a great dog. We had him for 9 years until he got sick and the sad day came, when we had to have him put to sleep. His ashes rest in peace under the apple tree and I remember him fondly.

Without a dog life was empty. I even went so far as to borrow my neighbor's dog for walks, and before long we had adopted a retired Greyhound. But I am getting ahead of myself. Did I mention our duck and chicken breeding experiment? If you read the first chapter of this book, you will know by now, how I ended up with a wonderful pet duck for 10 years, 6 chickens and a year later with a male duck named Ralph.

The boys were by now very responsible, in any other way than pet care. Feeding live stock for longer than a week or so was asking the impossible. Yes, you guessed correctly, I got conned into letting them out in the early morning in all kinds of weather, sometimes near arctic conditions, provided them with fresh water and food, then tucked them in at night making sure everyone was accounted for: chickens and ducks of course, as well as the kids! Once in a while I could shame or sweet-talk one or the other son into cleaning out the duck pond or the coop (I accepted it gratefully in lieu of a birthday or Mother's day gift) and again, being the lover of animals I am, grew into the experience and became the official "Chicken Lady".

Returning to our adopted Greyhound whom we called Buck, due to his fawn-color, he was a pure joy. Being trained at the track he walked on a leash like a dream and the boys, as well as my husband, did not mind walking him on occasion. However, he too ended up my final responsibility and would have had a rather sporadic feeding and walking schedule if left up to them. There is something about Mothers which makes us steady and thus an easy target.

For his 14th birthday my younger son decided that he had always hungered for a parakeet, a bird he could talk to and which would perch on his finger. At great expense I purchased the most beautiful bird cage I could find, after all, a boy does not turn 14 every day, and went to the local pet store where this little green feathered creature gave me the eye. He liked me! Knowing what I knew by now that was important and so I took him home, with proper food, feeding apparatus and toys.

Altogether it ended up being a very expensive birthday gift. I should have absconded to a tropical island instead for a well deserved rest.

The relationship between the bird and my son was short-lived. It lasted approximately one entire week, since Ignatius, as he was named, stubbornly refused to talk within that time frame. I was told that I had purchased an inferior bird with a low IQ. We had Iggi for 7 years. Like all the other pets he ended up Mom's bird and bonded with me. He never learned how to talk but was a cheerful little fellow and I miss him a lot. What I do not miss is cleaning his cage or finding a home for him when we went away. Today his empty cage is filled with an ivy; definitely much easier to care for.

One of the absolutely greatest animal experiences my children introduced me to was "Gollum", the iguana. One Christmas vacation my oldest son returned from college with a surprise. He had purchased a terrarium and a little green iguana, which he assured me was absolutely paper-trained. Once I got over my initial fear I had to admit that he had a certain charm, being so very green and sitting on my lap one minute while hanging on the curtains the next. Apparently a pet in your dorm room was the latest rage and highly valuable to one's study habits. I learned to feed him fresh broccoli but never could get used to him feasting on live crickets. To an animal lover a cricket is a cute creature and deserves better. Each time my son returned from college Gollum had grown considerably and the bigger he got, the more it became apparent, that he was rather bad tempered. Also he forgot about being "absolutely" paper-trained and regularly made quite a stinky mess.

During semester vacations my son's room started to reek disgustingly, but then, by some freak of nature, my oldest son has no sense of smell and was not bothered in the least. Naturally the rest of the family was.

Meanwhile we had lost our beloved Greyhound Buck to bone cancer and adopted Morgan, another retired racer. Morgan is an ALAPHA dog and there was no way for him to coexist with Gollum. It all came to a head when my son moved out and decided to leave Gollum in our care for "just a little while", until he got settled in his new apartment. So here was Gollum, all alone in his confinement, and I started to feel sorry for him. One beautiful summer day I put on gloves and took Gollum, who by now was about 2 feet long and all muscle, into the little fenced-in garden off the family room to let him sit in our dogwood tree and catch some rays. He blended right in and really seemed to enjoy the fresh air, (I can fully understand why) as well as the warm sunshine. While I sat down with a good book he climbed a few branches higher and seemed to settle in. "No problem," I thought, after a little reading and reprieve for Gollum I would simply pick him off the tree limb and put him back into his terrarium. Then, all of a sudden and like a bolt of lightening, Gollum was gone and hiding in the tall weeds behind the house . I was horror stricken! What would I tell my son? I had promised not to take Gollum outside. My great compassion for everything that is alive had clouded my judgement once again. I ran into the house and grabbed an old black towel. Meanwhile I had learned a lot about iguanas. Allowing children to have pets is very educational, at least for mothers, and I knew by now that iguanas, if approached from the rear, cannot see you. My husband meanwhile was wondering what I, the one person in the family who gets bitten more often by deer ticks than your average deer, was doing in the tall weeds. When told of Gollum's escape he simply shrugged his shoulders and remarked : "Well, we are finally rid of him". Do you know any loving Mom who would give up so easily? No, I searched high and low, finally found him and approached him from the rear. Then I threw the towel over him and with all the strength I could muster, I struggled to hold the creature and succeeded in carrying him back into the house. My husband's remark: "You never cease to amaze me," felt good. It is the kind of thing a woman likes to hear from the man she has been married to for over 25 years. Anyhow, Gollum was back where he belonged. We made our son take him on the occasion of his next visit, threatening to deprive him of his inheritance otherwise and all is well.

At this point I am still stuck with 5 chickens and one male duck who thinks he is a chicken, as well as our beloved Morgan. After the chickens go to chicken heaven or wherever it is they go, that will be it.

Yes we will most likely always have a dog, but if I am fortunate enough to have grandchildren some day and they express interest in pet ownership, they will have to keep them at their house! I feel I have done my duty and to all you young mothers out there, I did have fun and yes, it was worth all the trouble!!!

LOVE POEM TO A
HUSBAND OF MANY YEARS

LOOKED AT OUR FLOWER BOX THE OTHER DAY,

AND TO MY GREAT SURPRISE,

I FOUND MYSELF THINKING OF YOU, MY LOVE.

THE BOX ITSELF, SO SIMPLE, STURDY, WEATHERED.

COMFORTABLE LIKE AN OLD FAVORITE SHOE,

THOUGH IN MY MENTAL EYES, YOU ALWAYS WILL LOOK 26, THE DAY WE MET, SO LONG AGO.

THEN, WHEN I MOVED MY EYES UP TO THE FLOWERS,

THERE WAS A GREAT PROFUSION THERE OF BEAUTY, TALENT AND ENDURANCE, AS WELL AS SOME CONFUSION,

THROWN IN FOR ADDED CHARM.

A GOOD BALANCE, ALL IN ALL, THIS GROWTH WHICH WILL,

AS TIME GOES BY, COVER THE WEATHERED BOX AND EVER MORE DELIGHT THE SENSES.

HOW MUCH ALIKE YOU ARE MY LOVE.

YES YOU AND THAT OLD FLOWER BOX INDEED HAVE MUCH IN COMMON.

FROM YEAR TO YEAR YOU ARE MORE WONDERFUL AND INTERESTING,

AND AS FOR ME, I'LL DO MY BEST TO KEEP THE WEEDS AT BAY.

MARTHA – THE RESIDENT GROUND HOG

Well, I don't quite know how to tell you about Martha. I guess I best start at the very beginning. Three years ago I suddenly noticed a suspicious looking hole and a mess of dirt by the deck which surrounds the swimming pool. Then one day I saw her grazing peacefully in the front yard. After discussing the matter with my husband we decided MARTHA was a good name for our new arrival, and for a few days we rejoiced in having attracted yet another one of God's creatures to our 5 acre homestead in the Kittatinny Mountains of New Jersey. Plus she was cute, and we soon found out that she was the mother of three adorable little groundhogs.

Cheerfully I went out in the spring to plant my annuals in front of the house, as well as various other places in the back by the swimming pool. Since my surgery I had to give up on serious vegetable gardening due to physical limitations, but we did plant some of our favorite vegetables in half barrels. So after planting $50 worth of flowers I was pleased with the results, only to return the next morning to, yes you guessed it, NOTHING. They do not have groundhogs in Germany where I grew up, and I had no prior experience with them. Naturally I was surprised and a little "miffed" to be honest, seeing all my pride and joy eaten to little green stumps. Friends recommended I kill her (out of the question) or get a large HAVAHART trap dropping her and her brood off miles away, but how could I be sure not to separate the family. So I simply gave up on my annuals for that year and looked forward to my perennial flowers, only to find out that other than Tansy, Physostegia, Bleeding Heart and Peonies nothing was safe any longer. My perennial flower borders continued to get thinner and thinner while Martha's girth expanded considerably and her youngsters developed into handsome teenagers.

Then, shortly after coming to terms with the flower situation, I noticed a conspicuous increase in the amount of chicken feed I was using for my 5 chickens and Bob the duck. Checking the chicken yard there were the tell- tale signs of "groundhog invasion", holes dug under the fence and eventually I caught her red-handed, sitting right in the feeding dish gorging herself on chicken layer pellets. When I tried to scare her away she simply looked up at me with trusting eyes and gave me a big winning smile, then went back to eating undisturbed. By now I was ready to declare war! I went to great lengths plugging up her holes around the chicken yard with rocks, only to find them removed again the next day. Then I left one pot of chicken feed inside the coop and one outside, to give the chickens a chance to eat. But Martha is smart. On rainy days she now ate inside and her girth kept enlarging, which, considering the obesity problem of the American population at large, fits right in. Conveniently the exit of her burrow leads right to the back of the pool within close proximity of the chicken yard, so Martha and her family enjoy the best of both worlds.

During the winter she hibernated and her offspring went to my neighbors' property, much to their "delight".

Like a faithful friend she was back the next year and produced more babies. Meanwhile a well-meaning friend of mine had given me a sign reading: "No Groundhogs – Dammit!" which I placed right next to her abode, but while she is smart in a "groundhog way", reading is not her thing or else she is the stubborn kind who enjoys a challenge. By now I had given up on annuals other than in my enclosed "SECRET GARDEN" and in flower pots on the deck, choosing only those she was not fond of. However, the chicken feed situation was getting totally out of hand. It was starting to seriously annoy me and her happy smile had lost it's charm. While I still felt happy to see her graze in the evenings on the front lawn, together with a multitude of deer and rabbits, seeing her in the chicken yard could make me extremely angry.

The next winter came, my chicken feed budget went back down to an acceptable level, and I wondered about the life expectancy of a groundhog. Apparently it is longer than three years, because this spring Martha was back, more brazen than ever before. One morning my husband came into the house white as a sheet and I was fearing the worst: an imminent heart attack! But it was all Martha's doing. When he had lifted the hood of the truck to check the oil, guess who was sitting right on the engine with an impressive welcoming smile? Yes, Martha found another favorite place to hang out. Since then I don't get into the pick-up truck in the morning any longer prior to lifting the hood.

Now a lot of you folks probably shake your head and wonder why I put up with Martha. Frankly, I have become fond of her, even though she eats my flowers, vegetables and chicken feed. This has become her home. She is one of God's creatures and I have this soft spot in my heart for all of them. So I let nature take it's course, enjoy my menagerie of wild animals ranging from Bruno, the 450 pound black bear (although I respect him greatly) to deer who eat my fruit right off the fruit trees, rabbits, turtles, fox, opossum, raccoons, bats and all types of birds - the other evening I saw the largest owl I have ever seen swooping right overhead- and consider myself fortunate to live in the country with appreciation for all it has to offer, even if at times Martha can still make my blood boil. What the heck, she has to live somewhere and if she enjoys living here, so be it. Her e-mail address is martha@groundhog.com just in case she receives any mail ☺.

DOWSING – A GIFT OR A SUPERSTITION? THE PROOF IS IN THE WATER

About five summers ago, while still attending High School, my younger son worked at a FRUIT FARM during the summer months. The owners Mr. and Mrs. Best grow apple, pear and peach trees on their 57 acres, as well as seasonal vegetables and flowers of the finest quality.

One late afternoon, when I arrived to pick up my son, Mr. Best happened to be outside. When he saw me he approached the car and asked if my son had told me about dowsing for water. I had heard about the ancient way of finding water, had even seen a segment on a television program, but being rather skeptical, had never given it much thought and dismissed the whole idea as being an old wives' tale. By then I had been in the building business for almost 15 years and watched over many a well driller seemingly going to the "center of the earth".

So when Mr. Best asked if I was interested in seeing for myself how it worked I readily agreed. He held a freshly cut forked tree branch from a peach tree and asked me to place my hand next to his on one of the branches while walking alongside him, holding on tight. As we were approaching a certain area the branch in my hand began to twist and move perceptively. "You are not holding on tight", I was told, so I increased my grip until my knuckles turned white but the branch continued moving. At a certain location the end of the fork pointed straight to a spot on the ground. I was astounded to say the least. "This is where the water vein comes closest to the surface", I was told, "and where the most water can be found." Then he showed me that when we went beyond this particular point and backtracked, the branch would actually flip backwards, again pointing at the same spot it had done before.

Little did I know that Mr. Best is regularly called in by the State when new wells are drilled in State Parks. Laughingly he told of a trip out West to visit close friends in Lander, Wyoming. They had purchased a property in Din Witty Canyon along the Win River on the Shoshone Indian Reservation. His friends said: "Please don't find any oil, we need water which is more valuable out here." Needless to say water was found! "How do you do it, I inquired?" "Not everyone can," I was told, "it has to do with your electromagnetic field and I did not know I had this gift until I was in my twenties." Never known to be timid I asked if I could give it a try. He handed over the forked branch and to my great amazement I could almost immediately sense the movement and pulling in my hands as I was nearing the vein of water. Sure enough, at the same location as before the "crotch" of the branch pointed straight down. I looked at Mr. Best and he at me. "You are going to put me out of business", he said jokingly, "you have the gift". We laughed, I thanked him for the experience and went on my way home.

That evening my curiosity got the better of me. From my own apple tree I cut a forked branch about the size I had held that afternoon and walked over our land. It was no joke. I detected 3 major veins of water crisscrossing the property and strangely the strongest one led me right to our well, which is 140 foot deep and has a flow of 60 gallons per minute. We had been lucky!

My husband as well as both of my sons tried, but I am the only one in the family who can dowse. Over the next few weeks and months I sharpened my skill, and heaven only knows what the neighbors must have thought, seeing me wandering around the property with an outstretched branch in my hands. However, the feeling of being able to do and experience something which very few people can is quite wonderful, and I am very glad that I discovered this talent.

The next time a house we were building required a well, I asked Mr. Best to find the proper location. The future homeowners were "non-believers" until they themselves walked along and felt the powerful pull. Most people whose wells we dowsed for have kept the rod and are very excited about the novel experience. Even though I still called in the expert, (Mr. Best would write on a business card the depth and flow he anticipated and was always correct within a few feet or gallons), I started to explore the site myself prior to his arrival and would mark the spot I found with a simple rock. Soon it became very apparent to me that I would find the same location or usually be only a foot or so away from it.

From then on the well driller referred to me jokingly as the "water witch", since I would tell him exactly where to drill.

Our biggest success story led us to a home we were building in White Township, where a young couple was starting an ostrich farm, and of course a good well was very important to them. All surrounding neighbors had gone in excess of 700 feet with a minimal flow, but we ended up finding a well 160 feet deep with over 40 gallons a minute. They were very happy to say the least. I heard that since then Mr. Best has been called back to the area for more dowsing and people actually had new wells drilled.

Apart from the financial reward and savings for the customers, for me the much bigger reward is the feeling I experience when the natural elements respond to me or I to them, and I know from talking to Mr. Best that he feels pretty much the same. Both of us consider our ability a God-given talent. It is difficult to describe and I am happy that it confirms my connection to the earth and to nature. Likewise I am glad that there are still things, which cannot be explained by science.

How boring a world it would be if there were no more surprises of this kind, laughing in the face of the "computer age". Given my experience on many occasions there is no question in my mind, DOWSING is a precious gift!

HORSE NIBBLES

Truthfully, horses have never been my favorite animals. I have always appreciated their grace and beauty, but other than the gentle Belgian draft horse I knew as a child, I was afraid of them. I must have been about 4 years old, when the farmer next to us one day placed me on the back of the huge Belgian horse which pulled his plow, and I remember that my little legs stuck straight out from the sides of his wide back. It must have been quite a sight, since the farmer had a hearty laugh about it. I felt like I was riding an elephant and at the time, maybe I was just too young to be afraid.

About 5 years later though, while playing with my friends in the woods near our house, I watched a mother and daughter on horse-back. All of a sudden, the daughter's horse got spooked and took off at great speed, with the screaming girl, who could not have been older than myself, clinging on to the horse's neck desperately. That incidence scared me so much, that for the next 45 years I stayed clear of horses.

But then Arson and Sweety entered my life, and now I cannot wait while taking my daily walk to see "my" horses. Once Mrs. Parke passed away at the ripe old age of 92, her farm was purchased by a gentleman farmer and we have become friends. A few years ago he purchased two beautiful retired race horses, a mare named Sweety and a stallion named Arson. Both are large horses and at first they greatly intimidated me. During my walks I would frequently stop and admire them frolicking in the field, chasing each other through spring meadows, napping at lunch time or rolling on their backs with their legs sticking straight up in the air. Eventually I had to admit to myself that I was hopelessly hooked and my fear vanished.

Apple season came and I would never leave the house without plucking a few juicy apples from our trees, sticking them in my pockets and slowly but surely I was able to entice the horses to take the apples from my hands. Sometimes I had to call and coax them, since they were at the other end of the meadow, but pretty soon they began to recognize me, so it took less and less time for them to come and be rewarded with their treats.

Having seen a movie about horses, I gently blew into their nostrils and they recognized me after that. It really worked, and they would wait for me to take in my scent prior to accepting their treats. Now I was fascinated.

Sweety is a real lady, a beautiful animal, light brown with a black stripe running all the way down her back. She is friendly and gentle, always on the lookout for Arson's reaction, since he is the jealous type. Yes, Arson, a powerful stallion can be quite possessive, funny enough not of her but feeling deprived of my attention. Then he will make a threatening move towards her, and I have even seen him giving her a nibble on the rump that was definitely not a "love nibble".

Nevertheless Arson has become my special horse friend. Somehow he has taken to me more than anyone else, and when I approach the farm these days on my walks he comes running towards me. For some unexplained reason he loves my perfume, I use Patchouli Oil, and he insists on sniffing my right hand as long as I will let him. He almost seems to prefer the scent to the apple. Now that it is winter and I walk with a large scarf wrapped around my neck, he will bury his entire huge head in my chest.

At some point in his life he must have been abused, because for several winters he refused to enter his stall or the barn, staying outside even during the most inclement weather. But time seems to heal all wounds, even with horses, and he has learned to trust humans again. Arson loves when I speak to him softly and stroke his face with warm hands, telling him what a beautiful and fine horse he is. He allows me to scratch him behind his ears, rub his eyes ever so gently; then when I leave he follows me and watches wistfully until I disappear from sight.

Although I always bring equal treats for Sweety, she seems to know instinctively that he has laid claim to my affection, and disappears after she has eaten her apples. Just recently Arson started to nibble on my winter jacket. Not biting it, just nibbling on it and since last week he has learned to keep me in his presence for a while longer. He gently gets a hold of my big scarf and holds me there, not letting go until he has had his fill of affection for that day. That's what I call a "love nibble"! We have formed a strong bond and I no longer am afraid of horses, at least not Arson.

A COUNTRY HALLOWEEN

Thanks to the ingenuity and enthusiasm of my two sons, our house and neighborhood have earned the great distinction of being the scariest by far and truly representative of the Halloween spirit.

When the boys were about 8 and 12 years old they started early on in October with their preparations. They fashioned ghosts out of old bed sheets, a ball and a long stick, then suspended them on sturdy wires high up in the tree branches above our country road. When the wind got a hold of them they would sway freely high over the street, so that passing cars as well as neighbors quickly took notice and began to express their compliments on the flying goblins.

That encouragement was all it took. Next followed dummies made of worn-out clothes stuffed with leaves and hay. They were draped over tree branches at the entrance of our driveway in rather grotesque positions.

Meanwhile, every day after school, sawing and hammering could be heard from our workshop, as the boys made gravestones and crosses, bearing the names of movie characters from horror films. Each year something new was added and word spread, that our house was definitely worth a visit on Halloween. Other children on the road also caught the spirit and started hanging up ghosts and dummies, realizing there was more to this holiday than receiving free candy.

Even when our oldest son went off to college, he would come home for several weekends and continued to assist in the preparation. With the ghosts flying high in the autumn winds, the dummies in place and the cemetery laid out, the final touches were added on Halloween afternoon. A path of brown paper bags filled with sand and candles showed the way to the front door. Then came the selective placement of our carved pumpkins. Since our home has a large greenhouse along the entire front, the scariest jack-o'-lanterns were placed on the drying wood piles inside, and the stereo was wired to provide the appropriate sound effects. We had purchased a tape that played cackling witches, moans, squeaking doors, shrieks and eerie laughter. Now we were ready to go! After the boys had gotten into their often gruesome, home-made costumes, the fun could begin.

For a few years we were treated to a very special Halloween experience that just must be mentioned. Unfortunately it stopped once the young lady responsible for this great treat went off to college. She lived in the area and was the owner of a fine black horse. Just about sunset she would come riding down the road dressed up as the headless horseman. None of us will ever forget the sound of the horse's hooves on the pavement and the sight of her in costume without a head, carrying a lit jack-o'-lantern under her arm. It was truly wonderful and ranks near the top of some of our very best Halloween memories.

As it got darker the boys, my husband and I would light the candles in the bags and carved pumpkins, put on the audio tape and get into position waiting for "victims". One of us (we used to take turns) would sit in the greenhouse lit by nothing else but pumpkins. Dressed up as a dummy we would sit quietly with a tray of candy on our lap. As the parents accompanying little children and those kids, who were old enough to go out "trick-or-treating" alone came down the path, we could hear their laughter. Then, just as they reached the front door, one of us positioned behind it would open the door ever so slowly and whisper invisibly from our hiding spot: "The candy is on the dummies lap." Depending on age and courage the children would come closer and, after conquering their fear, snatch a piece of candy with a certain amount of trepidation. At that very moment the "dummy" would come to life and quickly grab their hand. Following the initial expression of fright, screams and then laughter from them as well as their parents, there were always positive comments on our display and performance.

From year to year our reputation spread by word of mouth, since the parents also enjoyed themselves and never failed to remark on the wonderful pumpkin carving skills our younger son had developed. Neighbors started bringing friends and relatives. To our great delight it had become a special yearly event to look forward to. We would vary our approach as to the dispensing of candy, in order to keep the kiddies in suspense and they loved it; creating memories for all of us to cherish and stories which will probably be told about the special "Halloween House" on Valley Road to future children and grandchildren.

The day after Halloween, all the pumpkins would be carried to a special corner of the yard and deposited in the "official" pumpkin cemetery, where they provided food for the many animals that frequent our place.

My sons fortunately grew up believing that there was more to Halloween than going from door to door getting free candy. Autumn was and still is their favorite time of year and Halloween was the highlight, scary, creative and fun!

I can imagine how they will tell their children about their adventures, and I hope that my future grandchildren will learn from them to get into the same spirit of a long- standing family tradition. In the meantime I take out my old Halloween photo album and smile, as I relish the countless memories we fashioned for others and ourselves. There is nothing like a good old-fashioned country Halloween.

SNOW WALKS

Somehow I don't quite remember when they started, just that the boys were still young and loved to go out on a bitterly cold, snowy night. At some point they enticed my husband and me to join them during a blizzard for a walk along our country road, and that was the beginning of a well established family tradition. For years now we love to hear a heavy snow storm is heading our way, since that will inevitably lead to one of our beloved snow walks.

Usually we wait until 9 or 10 o'clock at night, and by then the sloped glass in the front of our passive solar house is covered with snow, as are the skylights. It is bitterly cold. The winds are blowing snow in every direction, and that is when we all get bundled up to head outside into the winter fury and magic. Once we reach the street total quiet engulfs us. There are no cars on the road, and just the warm lights from inside our neighbors' houses give us an indication that we are not in the wilds of Alaska.

In the beginning, when the boys were small, there would be much laughter. They would throw themselves into snow-banks with total abandonment, make snow angels in the middle of the street or pelt each other (and us) with snow balls. However, as they grew older we would walk quietly, listening to the howling of the wind and the creaking of the tall trees which line our street. We would talk softly or not at all, just taking in the beauty of the wild winter elements.

By the time we would reach Parke Road and the Schwab sisters' grove of huge pine tees, our legs would start to get tired. The boys would find little snow caves below the tall pines, imagine they were stranded and rest a bit on the thick bed of pine needles. Then we would head up Parke Road until we reached old Mrs. Parke's farm and outbuildings.

There was always a light burning outside and the old farm would literally show us the way. Usually we would stand by the barns for a while, admiring the old structures and watch the snow whirling by the light. Nothing in the world could look more inviting than that old farm, standing its ground for yet another year against the inclement weather. We knew that inside, old Mrs. Parke would be sitting by her wood-burning stove with Shep, her old dog, and the mischievous tabby curled by her feet.

A little further up the mountain our legs would finally give out. We would turn around facing the stinging snowflakes, which would hit us now full force on the way down. Often, looking over the fields which surround Parke farm, we would share our feelings about how snow is the "great obliterator", that changes everything temporarily without changing anything permanently. Slowly we would walk back and again pass the beautiful tall pines, which by now would be straining under the heavy load they were carrying. If tomorrow would be sunny, and it usually is after a major blizzard, there would be icicles hanging on the tips of the branches, glistening in the bright sunlight. They would remind me of my childhood and the glass icicles made by my father after the war, which used to trim our Christmas tree in Germany back then.

Never once on our snow walks did we meet up with another human being, which made our excursions all the more special. By the time we finally made it home, we were ready for hot tea and hot chocolate, tired but feeling alive and happy to the core gathered around our own warm stove.

One has to venture outside in order to appreciate certain things, and all of us agreed that taking our snow walks constituted one of our favorite winter pleasures. As a matter of fact, a "good" winter for the family entailed at least half a dozen snow walks, while a winter with merely one or two was considered a "bad" winter.

As the boys grew older and one by one left for college, my husband and I were left to take snow walks alone. We missed the kids, and although we still love to venture out during a blizzard, without them it is just not quite the same. However, we feel good having had these magical times together and teaching them the beauty which is out there, even in the midst of the most adverse conditions. It may lead them to understand some of life's other lessons: that even in the center of the storm you can be steadfast and find some pleasure or positive aspect in just about any circumstance. Hopefully some day they will continue the tradition of snow walks with their own families and take their children out into the white magic.

THE CHRISTMAS CHURCH

Christmas, the most cherished holidays of Christians worldwide, took on a new dimension for my family a few years ago, when we attended the most meaningful Christmas Service in a very old Methodist Country Church not far from our home.

As far as the memories of outstanding Christmas celebrations that we fashion over the years are concerned, most people seem to favor those spent with small children, and while I treasure those as well, the memory of the very special Christmas service I am about to share with you, stands far above any other I have had.

About 5 years ago we found out, that the small and very old Methodist Church about a mile and a half from our home, was having a Christmas celebration on Christmas Eve. While the Church itself was no longer used on a regular basis and needs a lot of work, former members of the congregation had decorated it the night before with a beautiful Christmas Tree, red Poinsettias and pine branches in the deep window wells on either side of old-fashioned white candles.

We decided to go as a family with our two college-age sons, even though we are not Methodists, and attend the service in this Country Church. None of us will ever be able to duplicate the experience, nor would we want to, and I could see that even our youngest son was being drawn into the spirituality of the event.

A light snow had fallen that day, just an inch or so, and prior to leaving soft white flakes started to descend again. Since the way to the Church is uphill and I was just recovering from surgery, my husband and I drove, while the boys walked through the blustery night. Pulling up in front the Church looked very inviting, with big wreaths on the red door and the candle light shining softly through each window.

None of us had expected a great turnout, but to our great surprise we found ourselves in the company of most of our neighbors, members of a great variety of denominations, and the atmosphere could not have been any more congenial and festive.

Of my family I was the only one to ever having been inside the Church prior to this visit, but even I marveled once again at the beautiful craftsmanship of the rounded pews, the simplicity but thought provoking beauty of the altar and the charming stone work of the structure itself. The Minister, fully aware of the presence of a congregation from various backgrounds, held a wonderful Christmas sermon and the old-fashioned Christmas songs, accompanied by the organ, brought the old Church back to life, the way it must have been over one hundred years ago.

In over 50 years I had never felt the true Christmas spirit the way I did that cold snowy night. Near the end of the service candles were handed out to each person, the lights were dimmed and the sounds of " Silent Night, Holy Night" came straight from every person's heart. It seemed as though all of us were truly under the spell of the Christmas Miracle.

Before ending the church service, the congregation was called upon to share a special Christmas feeling. To my recollection everyone spoke up and expressed their joy, happiness and good will toward their fellow man. Since most of us knew each other, there was much happy laughter and exchanging of wishes for a Merry Christmas when leaving this wonderful event, and ever since, although the building was sold two years ago, to those who were present that night, it will always be remembered as "The Christmas Church".

TREE OF LIFE

PAST SAPLING, PAST MATURITY,

STILL REACHING UPWARDS, OUT,

NOT SURE FOR WHAT AT TIMES.

CONFUSED AND VULNERABLE,

WHILE OLDER BRANCHES GETTING BRITTLE,

ROOTS FRIMLY ANCHORED TO THE EARTH

AND NEW GROWTH RESTLESS IN THE WINDS OF AUTUMN.

MISUNDERSTOOD SO OFTEN, BY ACORN SPROUTS

NOT YET AWARE OR UNWILLING TO HEAR, THAT

OAK STILL DREAMS, THE ONES LEFT UNFULFILLED

WHILE TIME IS RUNNING OUT.

DREAMS TO SOAR AND TO DISCOVER

NEW VISTAS AND NEW HEIGHTS,

ALLOW TREE IT'S OWN FREEDOM, RIGHT TO DREAM,

DON'T STIFLE PRECIOUS GROWTH OR TREE WILL WITHER,

LOST TO THE WORLD, A VOICE THAT SPEAKS DIRECTLY

FROM THE HEART.

Inge Perreault

ABOUT THE AUTHOR

INGE PERREAULT is a writer with enormous reach and diversity. Whether she writes poetry or prose, short stories based on fact or fiction, newspaper commentaries with a keen sense of humor and social criticism, the most important fact shining through is her passion for the relevant subjects.

She was born and raised in a country setting in Europe and through her grandparents and parents developed a love of nature that has only deepened in the ensuing years as she raised her own children. Having written for various national publication, periodicals and newspapers, the response she received from readers, encouraged her to combine some of these short stories in her first book. The title says it all!

Inge Perreault can be reached at www.ingeperreault.com

www.ingramcontent.com/pod-product-compliance
Lightning Source LLC
Chambersburg PA
CBHW051437280526
45785CB00003B/1324